A Note to Parents & Teachers—

Welcome to I See Animals from Xist Publishing! These books are designed to inspire discovery and delight in the youngest readers. Each book features very simple sentences with visual cues to help beginners read their very first text.

You can help each child develop a lifetime love of reading right from the very start. Here are some ways to help a beginning reader get going:

- Read the book aloud as a first introduction
- Run your fingers below the words as you read each line
- Give the child the chance to finish the sentences or read repeating words while you read the rest.
- Encourage the child to read aloud every day!

Published in the United States by
Xist Publishing
www.xistpublishing.com
24200 Southwest Freeway
Suite 402-290
Rosenberg, TX 77471

First Edition

eISBN: 978-1-5324-1415-2
Saddle Stitch ISBN: 978-1-5324-1486-2
Perfect Bound ISBN: 978-1-5324-4208-7
Hardcover ISBN: 978-1-5324-3405-1

PUBLISHED IN TEXAS

I See Animals

Ferret

written by **August Hoeft**

xist Publishing
INSPIRING DISCOVERY & DELIGHT

I see a ferret.

The ferret
is black
and white.

The ferret has a long body.

The ferret
eats meat.

The ferret
lives in
the forest.

I see a ferret.

Things to do next!

Write a Sentence

I see a ________________.

Drawing

Make a drawing of
your favorite animal.

Sharing

Talk to your classmates about
your favorite picture in this book.
Explain to them why you like it.

WORD LIST

a
and
black
body
eats
ferret
forest
has
I
in
is
lives
long
meat
see
the
white

XIST PUBLISHING
INSPIRING DISCOVERY & DELIGHT